Wrestling Greats

RIC FLAIR

Ross Davies

 The Rosen Publishing Group, Inc.
New York

Published in 2001 by The Rosen Publishing Group, Inc.
29 East 21st Street, New York, NY 10010

Copyright © 2001 by The Rosen Publishing Group, Inc.

First Edition

All rights reserved. No part of this book may be reproduced in any form without permission in writing from the publisher, except by a reviewer.

Library of Congress Cataloging-in-Publication Data

Davies, Ross.
Ric Flair / by Ross Davies.— 1st ed.
p. cm. — (Wrestling greats)
Includes bibliographical references (p.) and index.
ISBN: 978-1-4358-8752-7
1. Flair, Ric, 1949——Juvenile literature. 2. Wrestlers—United States—Biography—Juvenile literature. [1. Flair, Ric, 1949– 2. Wrestlers.] I. Title.
GV1196.F59 D38 2001
796.812'092—dc21
                                                                  00-013232

Manufactured in the United States of America

Contents

1 Better Than Ever 5
2 The Young Rebel 12
3 The Courage of a Champion 18
4 Champion of the '80s 23
5 The Four Horsemen 33
6 Sting, Luger, and the Greatest Challenge of All 48
7 The WWF 61
8 Hogan Vs. Flair 75
9 Stylin' and Profilin' 84
Glossary 95
For More Information 102
For Further Reading 105
Index 110

With his stylin' and profilin', Ric Flair brought razzle-dazzle the once businesslike professional wrestling arena.

Better Than Ever

Ric Flair was back. Everybody could see that. He looked exactly the same as he did before, with his bleached blond hair, tanned and muscular upper body, and a smile that told people, "I'm the best." He was stylin' and profilin', as always. But the question remained: Was this Ric Flair the same man who left World Championship Wrestling (WCW), formerly the National Wrestling Alliance (NWA), nearly two and a half years ago?

There was reason to wonder. Although Flair had won two world championships during his two-year stay in the World Wrestling Federation (WWF), he had been dominated in his feud with Hulk Hogan. Flair hadn't exactly left the WWF on his own terms. In January 1993, he lost a loser-leaves-the-WWF bout to Curt Hennig. Since returning to WCW early in 1993, he had been unable to win the WCW world title from Big Van Vader.

That was no small matter to a man used to winning world titles wherever he went. The forty-four-year-old Flair was a nine-time former WCW world champion.

Counting his WWF titles, he had won eleven world championships, more than any other wrestler in history. Flair liked to say, "If you want to be the man, you've got to beat the man." By any measure, Flair had been the man for twelve years.

Now, however, Vader was the man. He had dominated WCW since winning the title in March 1993. He had seriously injured several of his challengers, including Cactus Jack. At Battlebowl on November 20, Vader and manager Harley Race attacked Flair during a battle royal. Flair was carried off on a stretcher. "That was just the beginning," Vader vowed. "Ric Flair hasn't begun to realize how much pain I can inflict on him."

Immediately, promoters signed Vader and Flair for a rematch at Starrcade '93 on December 27, 1993. The occasion was the tenth anniversary of Starrcade, a supercard Flair had dominated throughout his career. He had won two world titles at Starrcades, and he planned on making this one memorable, too. "If Vader beats me, I'll quit wrestling forever," Flair said. "I'm not going to end up like Harley Race, wrestling far past my prime just to collect a paycheck. I don't need the money anymore."

Flair and Race had a long history together. At the first Starrcade in 1983, Flair defeated Race for his first world title. The loss effectively ended Race's reign as a great champion, although he wrestled for several more years. Flair, who privately respected Race, didn't want to finish his career the same way: as an over-the-hill former great who could no longer contend for the big belts.

A sellout crowd packed Independence Arena in Charlotte, North Carolina, for Starrcade '93. Although he was born in Minnesota, Charlotte had become Flair's adopted hometown. He and his wife lived there with their children. Although stars such as Steve Austin, Sting, and the Road Warriors

> "If Vader beats me, I'll quit wrestling forever."
>
> -Ric Flair

wrestled on the undercard, the fans were there to see Ric Flair.

Vader, ferocious as ever, dominated Flair for the first fifteen minutes. Vader slammed him to the canvas and screamed, "Quit, Flair, quit!" but Flair refused to concede. While the referee was preoccupied with Race, Flair slammed a chair over Vader's leg and head. Flair kept attacking Vader's left knee. Flair covered Vader for the pin. Race, trying to save his man, mounted the top rope and dove. Flair ducked out of the way, and Race landed on top of Vader.

Flair continued assaulting Vader and scored the pin twenty minutes, thirty-eight seconds into the match. He had won his tenth WCW world title. More important, his great career would continue. "This is a great moment in the career of a great wrestler," Rick Steamboat, Flair's longtime friend and rival, told reporters. "There was never any doubt that he's great. Now we know he's an all-time great. I'm just glad we're going to be able to watch him a little longer."

The roar of the crowd was deafening. As Flair returned to the dressing room with the championship belt strapped around his waist, wrestling fans knew this great champion would walk that aisle once again. He had answered all of the questions. Flair wasn't the same man who had left WCW two and a half years ago. He was better.

2 The Young Rebel

The man the wrestling world came to know as Ric Flair was born Richard Morgan Fliehr on February 25, 1949, in Edina, Minnesota. Edina is a suburb of Minneapolis, the largest city in Minnesota. His father was a prominent Minnesota physician. His mother was an author. Both were very involved in the theater. Their son, of course, would become the star of another kind of theater: the theater of sports entertainment.

The Young Rebel

Ric was a good student, an excellent athlete, and a big sports fan. One of his favorite sports was professional wrestling. In the 1950s and 1960s, as Ric was growing up, one of the biggest wrestling stars in the world was "Nature Boy" Buddy Rogers. Rogers wasn't just an athlete. He was a star, and the ring was his stage. Rogers was a bleached blond with a muscular body. He was cocky and arrogant. He strutted in the ring. He would do anything to win. His signature finishing move was the figure-four leglock, a

Buddy Rogers

move in which he tied up his opponent's legs like a pretzel, then applied painful pressure to the thighs. Ric idolized Rogers.

In high school, Ric played basketball and was the state high school wrestling champion in 1967. His parents had a lot of money, so they sent him to Wayland Academy, a private military school in Wisconsin. There, he was an outstanding football player. When he graduated, Ric attended the University of Minnesota on a football scholarship and played offensive guard. But school life wasn't for him. "I guess I've always been a rebel," Flair said. "It's not that I didn't respect my parents when I was growing up, but let's say I disagreed with what my folks wanted me to be."

After two years of college, Ric was restless. He dropped out of school and decided to become a professional wrestler. Ric wasn't the first University of Minnesota student to turn to wrestling. The school had turned out several mat stars, including Bronco Nagurski and Verne Gagne.

Luckily, one of Ric's college classmates was Greg Gagne, whose father, Verne, ran a wrestling camp in Minnesota. Flair earned a spot in Verne Gagne's 1972 class and impressed his teachers right away. Flair was one of the most talented athletes Gagne had ever seen in his camp. Gagne was a nine-time American Wrestling Association (AWA) world champion and one of the greatest technical wrestlers.

Under the guidance of Gagne and professional wrestler Billy Robinson, Flair learned his trade. On December 10, 1972, he made his professional debut and wrestled to a draw with "Scrap Iron" George Gadaski. The Ric Flair who wrestled that night looked a lot different from the Ric Flair we know now: He had close-cropped brown hair and was a bit heavier.

Flair wasn't a patient young man. The son of wealthy parents, he was used to getting what he wanted. His opponents didn't pose much of a challenge, so he got bored. Verne Gagne, his straight-as-an-arrow teacher, was the exact opposite. "He could tell right from the start that he was losing hold of me," Flair said. "Gagne knows wrestling as well as anybody, but our personalities and style are so different."

In the middle of 1974, Flair left Minneapolis, went to North Carolina, and signed a contract with Jim Crockett Promotions. Jim Crockett Promotions was part of the National Wrestling Alliance (NWA), the most powerful wrestling federation in the world. Crockett was looking to expand and thought Flair could be a star.

Flair, who weighed 260 pounds for his pro debut, dropped to 240 pounds. He bleached his hair blond. He borrowed the nickname of his favorite wrestler, Buddy Rogers. He demanded that he be known as "Nature Boy" Ric Flair. He would never dishonor the name.

3 The Courage of a Champion

In the 1970s, wrestlers such as Harley Race, Dory Funk Jr., Jack Brisco, and Terry Funk dominated the National Wrestling Alliance. They were tough, talented wrestlers who took no nonsense from anybody. Other than their names, however, there wasn't much to distinguish one man from the other. Wrestlers weren't expected to be flamboyant. They were simply expected to get into the ring and win their matches. That's what these guys did.

Ric Flair, however, was different. His blond hair and his nickname set him apart from the others. Then there was his arrogance. He didn't walk to the ring. He strutted. He played to the crowd. After he said or did something he was especially proud of, he would howl, "Whooooo!"

He could wrestle, too. His amateur background and training at Gagne's school had paid off. Flair seemed to know every move in the book, from suplexes and knee-drops to punishing chops and his figure-four leglock. Flair was an instant hit in the Mid-Atlantic region, which stretches from Maryland to Georgia.

On July 4, 1974, he teamed with Rip Hawk and beat Paul Jones and Bob

Bruggers for the Mid-Atlantic tag team title. Less than a year later, Flair won his first singles championship when he pinned Paul Jones for the NWA TV title. Wrestling magazines began to notice Flair when he beat Wahoo McDaniel for the NWA Mid-Atlantic heavyweight title on September 20, 1975. At the time, the Mid-Atlantic heavyweight title was one of the most important championships in the sport.

Flair was living the good life. He ate in the finest restaurants, stayed in the best hotels, and flew in private planes. That last luxury almost cost him his life. On October 4, 1975, Flair, several other wrestlers, and a Jim Crockett Promotions official boarded a Cessna 310 plane in Charlotte, North Carolina. They were headed to a card that night in Wilmington, North Carolina.

At about 6:25 PM, as the plane approached a runway west of the Wilmington airport, the pilot radioed the control tower that one of his engines had stopped. The plane cut across treetops and snagged a wing on a utility pole before crash-landing a mile and a half from the airport.

Several occupants were thrown from the plane. Another was pinned between the seats. Two occupants suffered only minor cuts and scratches, but others weren't nearly so lucky. The pilot was killed. Flair's back was broken in three places.

Later, doctors told him it would take at least a year for his injuries to fully heal. A year seemed like an eternity to Flair, who was finally making headway in wrestling. Then he found out the really bad news: A doctor told him he should never wrestle again. His back injury was so severe that another injury could cripple him for life.

Though crestfallen, Flair refused to give up hope. He was treated by the best doctors. He underwent physical therapy. "I'll be back," Flair vowed. He was true to his word. On February 1, 1976, only four months after the accident, Flair returned to the ring and beat Wahoo McDaniel. During the first four years of his career, Flair had displayed his arrogance and confidence. This time, he showed his remarkable courage.

Champion of the '80s

By the middle of 1976, Ric Flair was achieving his fondest dreams. He had been named rookie of the year by *Pro Wrestling Illustrated*. On May 24, 1976, he beat Wahoo McDaniel for his second Mid-Atlantic title. He was making $125,000 a year and living in a beautiful house in Charlotte. He wore gold Rolex watches and diamond rings. Flair was the most stylish wrestler the sport had ever seen.

In the ring, Flair was all business. He and McDaniel feuded throughout 1976 and exchanged the Mid-Atlantic belt many times. On Christmas Day 1976, Flair and Greg Valentine beat Gene and Ole Anderson for the Mid-Atlantic tag team title. But Flair wanted more.

In 1977, Flair won his first world championship: He and Greg Valentine beat Gene and Ole Anderson for the NWA world tag team title. Over the next two years, he won several important singles titles, including the NWA TV title, and captured the national heavyweight title from Bobo Brazil, scientific-wrestling great Mr. Wrestling, and Rick Steamboat. On August 8, 1979, Flair and

Blackjack Mulligan won the NWA world tag team title.

Flair knew, however, that real fame and fortune weren't in tag team wrestling. They were in singles wrestling. If he wanted to be a superstar, he would have to win the NWA world heavyweight championship. "Nothing blinds me to the fact that in order to prove I am the best I must capture the world championship," Flair said.

His first order of business was proving to the world that he wasn't merely a cheap imitation of the original Nature Boy, Buddy Rogers. Rogers accepted his challenge, and on July 16, 1979, the Battle of the Nature Boys took place in Greensboro, North Carolina. Flair won with a figure-four leglock. Eight days later, he won a rematch.

But the world title remained elusive. Flair won—and lost—the national title several times, but he couldn't quite get his hands on the NWA world belt, held by Harley Race. Flair got his first break when Dusty Rhodes beat Race for the NWA title. On September 17, 1981, in Kansas City, Missouri, Flair stepped into the ring against Rhodes.

Rhodes, known as the American Dream, was one of the most popular wrestlers in the world. In 1978, the same year that Flair was named most hated wrestler of the year by *Pro Wrestling Illustrated*, Rhodes was named most

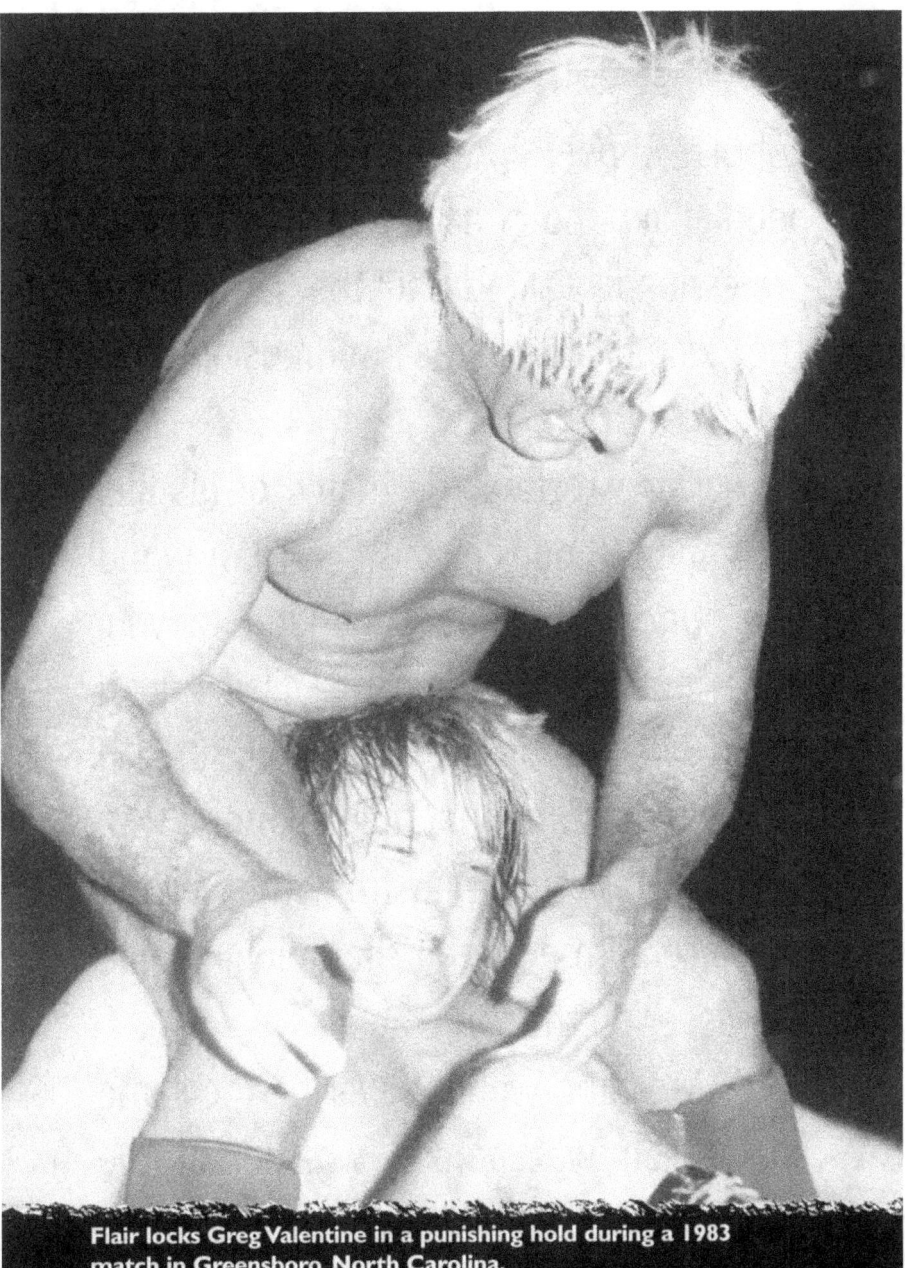
Flair locks Greg Valentine in a punishing hold during a 1983 match in Greensboro, North Carolina.

popular. Rhodes and Flair were both show people and both had started wrestling professionally at around the same time. They would cross paths hundreds of times in the 1980s.

Flair wrestled the match of his life. He pinned Rhodes for his first NWA world title. "Once that belt is handed to you, you're not the same person," Flair said. "I knew it as soon as that gold buckle touched my hand. The thought ran through my mind that from this second on, since I am now the champion, my life will never be the same again."

Wrestling would never be the same again. Flair was named wrestler of the year in 1981. He held on to the belt for

Champion of the '80s

two years before losing to Harley Race on June 10, 1983, in St. Louis, Missouri. That match would be named match of the year.

The most memorable match of 1983 occurred on the eve of Thanksgiving, November 24. The occasion was Starrcade, wrestling's first supercard. Before a crowd of 15,447 at the Greensboro Coliseum in North Carolina, Flair beat Race for his second NWA world title. Over the following years, Starrcade would become Flair's stage for greatness.

Flair was becoming wrestling's number one star and gate attraction. His feud with Race was thrilling. On March 21, 1984, Race won the title from Flair. Two days later, Flair won it back. Flair was discovering just how grueling it was to be world champion. Challengers came from all sides. On May 6, 1984, the crowd at Texas Stadium in Irving, Texas, watched hometown favorite Kerry Von Erich beat Flair for the title. Eighteen days later in Japan, Flair recaptured it. "Anyone who criticizes Ric Flair in any manner whatsoever had better think twice about what he says," Von Erich said.

"Flair's schedule is incredible, and I respect the man tremendously. I always have, but that respect is even greater now that I've had a taste of what being the world champion is all about."

For the second time, Flair held on to the world title for a long time. He was named wrestler of the year in 1984, 1985, and 1986. Although he lost the world title to Rhodes on July 26, 1986, he won it right back from Rhodes two weeks later. The experts, noticing Flair's habit of holding on to the NWA world title for a few years, losing it for a few weeks, and then winning it right back, suggested that Flair's periods without the belt were planned vacations.

"It's been like some sort of crazy battle royal or something, except that it's fifty against one," Flair said. "Fifty contenders against one champion. There's nothing like it anywhere else in sports, and it's a terrible amount of pressure to put on one man. If you're a contender, you can lose a match and there will always be tomorrow's match, or the next day's. For me, I can't afford to let my concentration lapse for even a second. If I lose, that's it, the whole championship goes out the window. It's a do-or-die situation each time I step into the ring." Fortunately for Flair, he always had plenty of help.

The Four Horsemen

R ic Flair had no shortage of friends. He lived fast. He drove fancy cars and often partied the night away after big victories. Among his friends were some of the toughest men in wrestling: Texan Tully Blanchard; manager James J. Dillon; and two of Flair's cousins, Ole and Arn Anderson.

Blanchard, Dillon, the Andersons, and Flair looked out for one another. If Flair was in trouble in one of his matches, he could usually count on one of the others to interfere on his behalf. The same was true of the Andersons and Blanchard, who were always in contention for the NWA world tag team title. One night, on the TV show *World Championship Wrestling*, the five men were gloating over injuring an opponent. Arn said, "The only time this much havoc has been wreaked by this few people, you need to go all the way back to the Four Horsemen of the Apocalypse."

The Four Horsemen were born. In later years, the New World Order (NWO) and the New Blood would become powerful forces in the NWA. Their forerunners were the Horsemen. The Four Horsemen

Flair was never afraid to taunt his opponents, especially when he had allies like Arn Anderson, Sting, and Ole Anderson to egg him on.

were a bunch the fans loved to hate. Their favorites were Dusty Rhodes, Magnum T.A., and the Rock 'n' Roll Express, who always seemed to be feuding with the Horsemen. At one point, all four wrestling members of the Horsemen held an NWA championship belt. But the main focus of the Horsemen was helping Flair retain the NWA world title.

They were successful. Flair's fifth NWA world championship reign lasted the rest of 1986 and well into 1987. The Horsemen were so single-minded in their quest that when Ole took time off to watch his son wrestle, the rest of the group fired him. In early 1987, Lex Luger joined the Horsemen and won the United States heavyweight title.

Once again, free time between title reigns didn't last long. On August 25, 1987, in Detroit, Flair lost the belt to fan favorite Ron Garvin. Flair wasn't worried. "He beat me tonight, but there is no way he'll ever do it again," Flair exclaimed. Garvin touted himself as the working man's champion, but he couldn't hold off

Flair dominated fellow Horseman Sting throughout his career.

Flair's challenge. Flair took a brief rest, then regained the belt from Garvin on November 26, 1987.

That same night, Luger lost the U.S. title to Dusty Rhodes and argued with manager J.J. Dillon. A few weeks later, Luger left the Horsemen. There would be many other Horsemen over the years, including Barry Windham, Sting, Sid Vicious, Chris Benoit, and Curt Hennig, but one member remained constant: Flair.

Flair feuded with every challenger in the NWA. Sting took a shot at Flair, but couldn't win the belt. Flair had a great series of matches with Luger, too. On July 10, 1986, Flair battled Luger at the Great American Bash in Baltimore, Maryland.

Late in the match, Luger raised Flair high above his head in a move called the backbreaker. Flair was about to submit when the bell rang. Blood trickled down Luger's forehead. A Maryland rule prohibited blood in the ring, so Luger was disqualified. "He got lucky," Luger said angrily. "That belt was mine."

Luger stepped up his quest for Flair's title. Former National Football League (NFL) star John Ayres was appointed special referee for several Luger-Flair bouts, but Flair retained the belt. "This has gone way beyond just wanting the title," Luger told *Pro Wrestling Illustrated.* "I despise Flair and everything he stands for." Flair

Flair shows no mercy to a vanquished Jim Garvin as he works on his opponent's leg during the Greensboro Bash of 1986.

replied, "Do you really expect me to worry about that punk?"

Why should Flair worry? Whenever he got into trouble, either the Horsemen or some obscure rule was there to save him. The fact was, a lot of people disliked Flair, and many people disrespected him, too. His arrogance was a turnoff. Flair did lose a lot of matches by disqualification and countout. That was fine with Flair, who could lose the world title only if he was pinned or submitted. Others, however, thought Flair was soiling the integrity of the belt. The Horsemen's constant presence made matters worse.

Although few people wanted to admit it, Flair was an outstanding wrestler.

The Four Horsemen

One of his most challenging rivalries was with Rick "the Dragon" Steamboat. Steamboat was one of the best wrestlers in the world. He had tremendous mat and aerial skills as well as seemingly endless stamina. He and Flair had been friends on and off for the past ten years, and they secretly respected each other.

Many people thought Flair was simply taking another vacation from being champion when Steamboat pinned him for the world title on February 20, 1989. Perhaps Flair was thinking the same thing. After all, Harley Race, Dusty Rhodes, Jim Garvin, and Kerry Von Erich had also beaten Flair for the belt, only to lose it shortly afterward. But when Steamboat

Flair pounded Rick Steamboat into submission, winning his sixth NWA world title, in Nashville, Tennessee, on May 7, 1989.

beat Flair in a best-of-three-falls match at Clash of the Champions VI on April 2, 1989, fans knew they were watching the Nature Boy's toughest test.

Flair and Steamboat had several more marathon matches. Most of them ended in time limit draws. On May 7, 1989, Flair and Steamboat met again at Wrestle War '89. In what would be known as his greatest match, Flair reversed a pin and beat Steamboat in thirty-one minutes, thirty-seven seconds for his seventh NWA world title. It was an honest and clean victory for Flair, who had matched moves with Steamboat all night. When the match ended, Flair and Steamboat shook hands.

Former NWA world champion Terry Funk was in no mood for a celebration. Before anyone knew what happened, Funk attacked Flair in the ring. The piledriver that Funk used to send Flair crashing through a wooden ringside table cracked vertebrae in Flair's neck and partially ruptured a disc in his back. Flair hadn't needed the Four Horsemen to regain the world title, but he could have used them once Funk arrived on the scene. He would be out of action for nearly three months.

6 Sting, Luger, and the Greatest Challenge of All

The Flair-Funk feud was extremely violent. Funk was a no-nonsense wrestler who took pleasure in crippling his opponents. He made no exception for Flair. On June 15, 1989, Flair and Funk battled in an "I Quit" match in Troy, New York.

This was a special night for Flair. He was honored by *Pro Wrestling Illustrated* as wrestler of the decade. When the bell rang, Flair outclassed Funk from start to finish. After twenty minutes, Flair caught Funk in a figure-four leglock. Funk

Although Lex Luger was one of Flair's most formidable rivals, he failed to best Flair in world-title matches.

screamed in pain and submitted. Afterward, Funk shook Flair's hand and conceded defeat. But then Funk was blindsided by his own manager, Gary Hart. Flair rescued Funk by battering Hart in the corner, but then two other wrestlers, the Great Muta and the Dragon Master, attacked Flair. Sting came to Flair's rescue. Flair put Muta in a figure-four leglock. Lex Luger came to ringside with a metal chair and bashed Sting. Then Luger left Flair lying unconscious in the middle of the ring. "I will never forgive Lex Luger for what he did tonight," Flair vowed.

Flair held off world title challenges from Luger and also beat Funk at the 1989 Great American Bash. At Fall Brawl '89, Funk tried to suffocate Flair with a plastic

Sting, Luger, and the Greatest Challenge of All

bag and was suspended. Flair was angry and wanted revenge. Flair paid the $100,000 fine to have Funk reinstated and available for a rematch. The '80s ended with Flair on top of the NWA. The '90s marked a new era for the Four Horsemen. In January 1990, Sting was named an official member of the group. "Sting is finally being rewarded for being one of the best wrestlers in our sport," Flair said.

But when Sting demanded a shot at Flair's world title, the Horsemen were enraged. They were even angrier when the NWA announced that Sting would get a shot at the world title at Wrestle War '90 in February. The Horsemen gave Sting until the end of the Clash of the Champions

Flair prepares for his finishing move against Sting in Starrcade '89.

match on February 6 to pull out of Wrestle War '90. Sting refused. Later, the Horsemen attacked him in a parking lot. Sting suffered a serious knee injury. "You did the one unforgivable thing that we can never forget," said Ole Anderson, who had returned to the Horsemen. "When you signed that match to meet Ric Flair on February 26, you signed your death warrant."

Sting was out of the way, and the NWA announced that Luger would replace him in the match against Flair at Wrestle War. Midway through the match, Sting hobbled to the ring on crutches to cheer Luger. Luger couldn't believe his eyes. He and Sting had been enemies for a long time. When Ole and Arn Anderson

attacked Sting, Luger came to his rescue. Luger was counted out of the match.

Flair and Luger feuded all over the United States. The Horsemen attacked Luger all over the country. Flair held on to the title. Then Sting returned to action at the Great American Bash on July 7, 1990, in Baltimore and pinned Flair for the world title.

Once again, most people expected Flair to win the title right back. Once again, they were wrong. In one three-week period, Sting pinned Flair eight times. At Starrcade '90, Sting pinned a masked wrestler called the Black Scorpion. The Black Scorpion was revealed to be Flair. But Flair couldn't be denied forever. On January 11, 1991, he beat Sting for his eighth NWA world title.

As 1989 NWA world champion, Flair strikes a triumphant pose for wrestling fans.

The NWA, however, was on the verge of a major change. Millionaire business mogul Ted Turner had purchased Jim Crockett Promotions, the largest member of the NWA, in November 1988. Turner's cable television station, TBS, broadcast World Championship Wrestling (WCW) programs that featured NWA stars. Over the months that followed, the lines between the NWA and WCW became blurred in the eyes of fans. In 1991, Flair was declared the first WCW/NWA world champion.

The name change didn't affect Flair's fortune in the ring. He continued to overcome challenges, including a tough match against Japanese champion

Tatsumi Fujinami. Outside the ring, however, Flair had problems.

Dissension was rocking the Horsemen. Flair had paid a huge bonus to Sid Vicious for joining the group, angering the other members. In April, the Four Horsemen split up, but Flair had other worries. His contract with WCW had expired.

He was shocked when the company wanted to cut his annual salary from $780,000 to $350,000. "I don't know how they could possibly expect me to accept their offer," Flair said. "Imagine a baseball manager walking up to Jose Canseco and saying, 'Jose, tomorrow we're going to cut your check in half.' Would they expect him to say, 'Oh, fine?' I'm stunned. I just talked to [WCW Executive Vice President] Herd two weeks ago and he said I'd be there the rest of my life. They had always called me their flagship wrestler."

When Flair refused to take the pay cut, WCW did the unthinkable: It fired him. On July 2, 1991, a press release was sent to the media with the headline, "Ric Flair and WCW to Part Company." News of Flair's firing shocked the wrestling world. Flair was, indeed, WCW's flagship wrestler. He was a nine-time world champion and five-time wrestler of the year. Other than Hulk Hogan, he was the most famous wrestler in the world. As it turned out, the surprises weren't over.

The WWF 7

By 1991, WCW was no longer the most popular federation in North America. For a long time, that designation belonged to the World Wrestling Federation (WWF). Riding on the amazing popularity of world champion Hulk Hogan, the WWF overshadowed WCW.

The two federations could not have been more different. While WCW concentrated on pure wrestling, the WWF was considered a circus by traditional wrestling fans. Hogan was considered a one-dimensional brawler who depended on kicking and punching to win his matches. Flair, on the other hand, was considered the finest all-around wrestler in the world. WCW was the opposite of the WWF. Flair was the opposite of Hogan.

But on September 10, 1991, Flair signed with the WWF. Flair made his WWF debut on September 10, 1991, in Cornwall, Ontario, and beat Jim Powers. Over the following weeks, he also wrestled Roddy Piper, with whom he had feuded in the NWA. Of course, what the fans really wanted to see was a first-time match between Flair and Hogan. For years, there had been talk of an interfederation match between Flair and Hogan.

The WWF refused to make a big deal out of the potential Hogan vs. Flair confrontation. After all the years of anticipation, their first meeting didn't occur at a supercard or as a pay-per-view TV broadcast. In fact, it wasn't aired on television at all. They met in Dayton, Ohio, on October 23, 1991, where Hogan lost to Flair by disqualification. Two days later in Oakland, California, Flair lost to Hogan by disqualification.

Flair made his WWF pay-per-view debut at the Survivor Series on November 27, 1991, where he teamed with the Mountie, Ted DiBiase, and the Warlord in

Flair and Terry Funk scramble for advantage during a cage match at the Thunderdome in Philadelphia.

Ric Flair

an elimination match against Roddy Piper, Bret Hart, Virgil, and Davey Boy Smith. Flair pinned Smith at the 10:55 mark, and his team won after 22:48 when the opposing team was disqualified.

But Flair wasn't finished for the night. Later, during the world title match between Hogan and challenger the Undertaker, Flair came to ringside and grabbed the championship belt. Hogan ran from the ring and blasted Flair with his right hand. Shortly afterward, the Undertaker prepared to piledrive Hogan while referee Earl Hebner argued with Paul Bearer, the Undertaker's manager. Flair slid a folded metal chair into the ring. The Undertaker piledrived Hogan onto the chair, then scored the pin to win the world title. "What did you think was going to happen?" Flair gloated. "When I arrived here, I told Hogan face to face that he was short-lived. And, by God, he is ... But now it's all over. There's one—just one—world heavyweight champion, and you've got to know it's me."

Well, not yet. During the Undertaker vs. Hogan rematch on December 3, Undertaker had Hogan locked in a claw. Flair strutted to ringside and argued with WWF president, Jack Tunney. Hogan blasted Flair with a chair. The blow sent Flair careening into Tunney, knocking him out. Paul Bearer tried to hit Hogan with an urn. Hogan ducked and Bearer hit Undertaker. Hogan threw ashes in Undertaker's face and pinned him for the belt. The next day, citing what had happened in the match, Tunney declared the world title vacant.

The world title was put up for grabs at the Royal Rumble on January 19, 1992, in Albany, New York. The Royal Rumble is a battle royal–type match in which thirty wrestlers enter the ring one at a time every two minutes. The object is to eliminate opponents by dumping them over the top rope. The last man standing is the winner. In this case, the last man standing would become the WWF world champion, too.

The odds were against Flair, who was the third man to enter the ring, but he wrestled the match of his life. Flair lasted sixty-two minutes, two seconds, a Rumble record for longevity. He eliminated the British Bulldog, Big Bossman, and Randy Savage, and he assisted in the elimination of eight others. After Flair combined with Sid Justice—the former Horseman who was known as Sid Vicious in WCW—to eliminate Randy Savage, only he, Justice, and Hogan remained.

When Hogan tried to eliminate Flair, Justice dumped Hogan over the top rope. Hogan and Justice argued. Hogan tried to pull Justice out of the ring. Flair got up, picked up Justice by the legs, and dumped him over the top rope. Flair became the WWF world champion.

Flair was the second man to win both the WWF and NWA/WCW world titles.

Randy Savage grimaces as he tries to escape one of Flair's punishing footlocks.

Appropriately, his idol, Buddy Rogers, was the first. "With a tear in my eye, this is the greatest moment in my life," Flair said. "This is the only title in the wrestling world that makes you number one. When you are king of the WWF, you rule the world."

Said Buddy Rogers to *Pro Wrestling Illustrated Weekly*: "I've always said that the only man today who comes close to what I did in the ring is Ric Flair. Just the fact that he took my name, Nature Boy, is very flattering to me." Flair's humility didn't last long. He was as arrogant in the WWF as he had been in WCW. "To be the man, you gotta beat the man!" Flair kept boasting.

Randy Savage kept trying to beat the man. Savage was furious when Flair claimed to have incriminating photos of himself with Savage's wife, Elizabeth. He got even madder when the photos were released for public viewing. Savage got revenge and won the world title at WrestleMania VIII on April 5, 1992, in Indianapolis, Indiana. A crowd of over 60,000 packed the Hoosier Dome for Flair's first WrestleMania appearance. Although Flair lost the title to Savage on that night, he would always remember the event for two reasons: the size of the crowd and the kiss he placed on Elizabeth's lips. Savage was even angrier than before.

Savage won several rematches. Flair interfered in Savage's world title defense against the Ultimate Warrior at the Summer Slam '92 contest. Flair thought he, not the Warrior, deserved the title shot. On September 1, 1992, in Hershey, Pennsylvania, Savage and Flair tore into each other again. Razor Ramon interfered in the match to Flair's advantage, and Flair won his second WWF world title.

Flair, however, had been worn down from his years as WCW/NWA world champion and his feud with Savage. Bret "the Hitman" Hart, an outstanding all-around wrestler from Canada, proved to be too much for the Nature Boy. On October 12, 1992, Flair submitted to the Hitman's "sharpshooter"—a variation of Flair's figure-four leglock—and lost the belt. Flair and Hart wrestled many times at the end of 1992, but Flair couldn't regain the title.

Success and controversy had marked Flair's time in the WWF. He would never forget his experience at WrestleMania. The matches with Hart were some of the best WWF fans had ever seen. He finally had the chance to wrestle Hogan. But a feud with Curt Hennig, Flair's former technical adviser, would mark the end of Flair's brief tenure in the WWF. On January 18, 1993, Flair lost a loser-leaves-the-WWF bout to Hennig. Flair's last match in the WWF was on February 10, 1993, in Dortmund, Germany. And then, the Nature Boy went home.

Hogan Vs. Flair

The fans in Ashville, North Carolina, on February 21, 1993, were there for SuperBrawl III. What they got was a welcome-home party. That night, Flair returned to WCW. Flair was introduced to the crowd and provided television commentary for one match.

Three months later, at Slamboree '93, Flair introduced the new version of the Four Horsemen: Arn Anderson, Ole Anderson, and Paul Roma. All four men wore tuxedos. "This is as much about image and attitude as it is about winning," Flair said. "Anybody can win a match. Only the Horsemen can do it right. A lot of people were wondering what took me so long to get back into the ring. The answer is, I wanted to do it right. That's the Horseman way."

Flair returned to the ring at the Clash of the Champions on June 17, 1993. He teamed with Arn Anderson and beat Brian Pillman and Steve Austin. "Rick has this world title hunger that even I can't explain," said Anderson. "Ric has to be the man, and he's not the man as long as someone else has the belt. Ric doesn't like that and neither do the rest of us. If the Four Horsemen are going to be together, then we have to be the best."

The champion was ferocious. Big Van Vader, who weighed 450 pounds, loved to hurt people with his favorite move, the powerbomb. Vader was managed by Harley Race, Flair's longtime rival. In the first meeting between Vader and Flair, Flair avoided the powerbomb, and Vader lost by disqualification.

During another Clash of the Champions match on November 10, 1993, Flair thought he had pinned Vader for the belt. But referee Randy Anderson disqualified Vader for accidentally hitting him. Flair won one rematch, then another. At Spring Stampede '94, Flair had another spectacular match against old rival Rick Steamboat. The match ended with both men's shoulders pinned to the mat.

Fans marveled as Hulk Hogan got the better of Flair in a bout at Madison Square Garden in 1991.

Right around that time, the eyes and ears of the wrestling world had turned to Hulk Hogan. Rumors circulated that Hogan was on the verge of leaving the WWF and jumping to WCW. For months, Flair and Hogan engaged in a war of words. On June 24, 1994, Hogan signed with WCW. "I've got some unfinished business with Ric Flair, the man who's won more world titles than anyone," Hogan said. "Well, if Flair wants a piece of me, he can have it. I'm ready any time."

Maybe the WWF didn't make a big deal out of Flair vs. Hogan, but WCW milked it for all it was worth. On July 17, 1994, Flair and Hogan got ready to step into the ring for their first WCW meeting. "Hogan could bring every one of his Hulkamaniacs, his entire family, and every sports hero he ever met to the ring with him, it wouldn't make a difference," Flair said."He still has to go toe to toe with me, the greatest wrestler in history. And I am the better man."

Well, not quite. Despite the assistance of manager Sherri Martel, Flair lost the title to Hogan, who pinned him in twenty-one minutes, fifty-three seconds. The Flair-Hogan feud intensified. During Clash of the Champions XXVIIII on August 24, 1994, Hogan was attacked by a masked man and clubbed in the knee while being interviewed. Refusing to concede the match, Hogan returned from the hospital to the arena and lost to Flair by countout. When

> "He still has to go toe to toe with me, the greatest wrestler in history. And I am the better man."
>
> -Ric Flair about Hulk Hogan

Flair, Martel, and the masked man attacked Hogan after the match, WCW commissioner Nick Bockwinkel suspended Flair and Martel. The suspension enraged Flair. He wanted nothing more than to destroy Hogan. Hogan wanted to destroy Flair as well. The intensity of their hatred for each other compelled them to put their careers on the line in a loser-must-retire match.

The steel cage match on October 23, 1994, at Joe Louis Arena was one of the most anticipated in wrestling history. Martel interfered on her man's behalf. Hogan clotheslined Flair. Flair chopped Hogan, who turned around and clotheslined him again. Martel charged at Hogan, who clotheslined her. Hogan backdropped Flair. Martel tried to get out of the cage. Hogan slammed her. Flair tried to leave the cage, but Hogan caught him and rammed him into the cage. Hogan scored with a flurry of punches and kicks that felled Flair, then covered him for the pin. Mr. T, the actor who served as special referee for the match, made the countout at 19:24.

For one of the few times in his life, Flair had failed to pass a test. This time, his career was over. "It was a great ride," Flair declared after the loss. "It's difficult to think of things to say right now." He really didn't want to say good-bye.

9 Stylin' and Profilin'

For twenty-two years, Ric Flair had been stylin' and profilin' in wrestling arenas around the world. He had beaten the best the United States, Canada, and Japan had to offer. Wrestling was his life. He simply couldn't walk away.

Although the Nature Boy honored his promise to not wrestle, he resolved his differences with Big Van Vader and managed him in a feud against Hogan. At the SuperBrawl V match, Flair interfered and kept the

Hogan-Vader match from reaching a definitive conclusion. "I'm back," Flair declared. "You haven't seen the last of me, Hogan!"

Hogan wanted revenge so much that he convinced the WCW executive committee to reinstate Flair. At Slamboree '95 on May 21, Flair and Vader teamed up against Hogan and Randy Savage. During the match, Flair, Vader, and Arn Anderson attacked Angelo Poffo, Savage's seventy-year-old father.

Now Savage wanted revenge, too. Flair knew, however, that the angrier his opponents got, the worse they wrestled. Flair had the upper hand throughout his feud with Savage, who was embarrassed by his inability to gain revenge for his father.

The ultimate embarrassment occurred at Starrcade '95, when Flair beat Savage to win his eleventh WCW/NWA world title belt.

Savage reached his low point on February 11, 1996. Three weeks earlier, he had regained the world title from Flair. But at SuperBrawl '96, the unthinkable happened: Elizabeth, now

Savage's ex-wife, handed Flair one of her high-heeled shoes. He used it to blast Savage and score the pin for his twelfth WCW world title. "I always knew Liz had it in her," Flair said. "Now she knows what it's like to be with a real man."

Flair, however, was getting older. On April 22, 1996, a rookie named the Giant—known in the WWF as the Big Show—chokeslammed Flair for the world title. The Nature Boy's body was breaking down, too. In September, Flair suffered a shoulder injury when he was thrown to the mat by Kensuke Sasaki. He underwent surgery to repair the torn rotator cuff in his left shoulder, and he had to take off for several months.

From the sidelines, Flair watched as the wrestling world changed. A new rule-breaking supergroup called the New World Order formed. Hogan, who had been a fan favorite for most of the past two decades, shocked everyone by joining the NWO.

On May 18, 1997, Flair returned to the ring at Slamboree. The crowd in Charlotte, North Carolina, greeted him with a thunderous ovation. Flair teamed with NFL star Kevin Greene and Roddy Piper to battle the NWO trio of Kevin Nash, Scott Hall, and Syxx. They won when Flair placed Hall in the figure-four leglock and scored the pin.

The NWO was Flair's biggest problem. Curt Hennig defected to the NWO just weeks after joining the Horsemen. On

September 29, 1997, unable to find suitable replacements for Hennig, Jeff Jarrett, and the retired Arn Anderson, Flair tearfully disbanded the Horsemen. One supergroup had been replaced by another.

With the Horsemen gone, 1997 was a down year for Flair. For the first time since 1980, he went an entire year without once holding a world title. The truth was, Flair didn't really care. He finally had time to spend with his wife and children. How could he have known that his children would be the cause of one of his greatest triumphs... and his greatest heartaches.

In April 1998, Flair was granted a leave from the WCW committee so he could watch his son Reid in a youth wrestling tournament. When WCW president Eric Bischoff, who also ran the NWO, found out what the committee had done, he demanded that Flair cancel his plans and wrestle. "Forget about it," Flair told Bischoff. He went to his son's wrestling match. WCW countered by suing Flair for $2 million for breach of contract.

For a good part of three decades, Flair had faithfully served WCW and the NWA. He had been the main reason for the NWA's return to glory in the early 1980s. This seemed like a shabby way to treat perhaps the greatest wrestler of all time. Flair was gone ... or so it seemed.

On September 14, 1998, Flair made a tearful return to WCW. He thanked the fans for their support and announced that the Four Horsemen were back together: Dean Malenko, Steve McMichael, Chris Benoit, and Arn Anderson. The hatred between Flair and Bischoff intensified. Flair turned up the heat. On January 4, 1999, Flair battled Bischoff for control of WCW for ninety days. Flair won. The wrestler was now the president of WCW.

Flair used his position to humiliate Bischoff. He forced him to do demeaning chores, such as cleaning arena bathrooms and setting up the ring. Bischoff, however, was still operating behind the scenes. On January 17, Flair's oldest son, David, made his pro debut at Souled Out '98. He teamed with his father and beat Curt Hennig and

Although he no longer dominates the sport, Flair wants the wrestling world to always think of him as its true champion.

Barry Windham. But after scoring the pin that enabled him and his father to win, David was savagely beaten by Hogan.

Nothing, however, could have prepared Flair for the heartache that followed. At SuperBrawl '99, David attacked his own father. The glory days were not yet over for Flair. But the feud with his son would overshadow all of these achievements.

In 2000, David joined the New Blood, an anti-old generation group led by WCW writer Vince Russo. He let the world know that growing up as the son of Ric Flair was a living hell. One night, David took WCW cameras on a tour of the family mansion and made a mockery of his father and mother's belongings, while pointing out that he never received the spoils that usually come with being a rich kid. His father, he claimed, had ignored him.

Ric Flair was torn. He didn't want to battle his own son, but his legacy was being challenged. He wanted the wrestling world to always think of the Nature Boy as a true champion. But Ric Flair should know better: Wrestling will always consider him one of its greatest champions.

Glossary

apocalypse A term originally from early Christian and Jewish writings. It refers to a cosmic disaster or final doom that is wildly unrestrained and during which the ruling powers of evil are destroyed.

armlock A move in which one wrestler pulls the opponent's arm behind his or her back by placing his or her arm between the opponent's arm and back.

backbreaker A submission move in which the wrestler lifts the opponent over his or her head by gripping the opponent's back.

card The list of matches on a wrestling show.

clothesline An offensive move in which the attacking wrestler sticks out one arm and uses it to strike the victim in the neck. The clothesline is often executed by whipping the opponent into the ropes, then striking him or her in the neck on the rebound.

contract A binding agreement or business arrangement between two or more persons or parties that is usually legally enforceable.

countout A wrestler is counted out if he or she is out of the ring for twenty seconds or more. When the wrestler leaves the ring, the referee begins the count at one. If the wrestler is counted out, he or she is disqualified.

crestfallen Having a drooping or hanging head from feeling shame or humiliation: dejected.

disqualification   In wrestling, a wrestler can lose by disqualification if he or she uses a foreign object, refuses to obey the referee's orders, breaks the rules repeatedly, is counted out of the ring, or if another person interferes on his or her behalf. Except in the event of a double disqualification—in which both wrestlers lose—the victory is awarded to his or her opponent. In most championship matches, the belt does not change hands on a disqualification, only on a pin or submission.

draw   A contest left undecided or deadlocked; a tie.

Glossary

figure-four leglock A move in which a wrestler ties his or her opponent's legs like a pretzel and then applies painful pressure to the thighs.

flagship The finest, largest, or most important one of a series, network, or chain.

flamboyant Marked by or given to strikingly elaborate and colorful displays or behavior.

manager The person responsible for overseeing a wrestler's inside-the-ring and outside-the-ring activities. Managers often take care of a wrestler's business affairs (such as signing contracts and arranging matches) and also assist with strategy.

pin When either both shoulders or both shoulder blades are held in contact with the mat for three continuous seconds. A pin ends a match.

promoter The person responsible for hiring and contracting the wrestlers for a card or federation. The promoter is also responsible for deciding the matchups for a card.

submission hold A move that makes an opponent give up without being pinned.

tag team match Match involving two teams of two or more wrestlers. Only one wrestler is allowed in the ring at a time.

For More Information

Magazines

Pro Wrestling Illustrated, The Wrestler, Inside Wrestling, Wrestle America, and *Wrestling Superstars*
London Publishing Co.
7002 West Butler Pike
Ambler, PA 19002

WCW Magazine
P.O. Box 420235
Palm Coast, FL 32142-0235

(904) 447-3462
Web site: http://www.wcw.com

WOW Magazine

McMillen Communications
P.O. Box 500
Missouri City, TX 77459-9904
e-mail: woworder@mcmillencomm.com
Web site: http://www.wowmagazine.com

Web Sites

Dory Funk's Web Site
www.dory-funk.com

Professional Wrestling Online Museum
www.wrestlingmuseum.com

Pro Wrestling Torch
www.pwtorch.com

World Championship Wrestling
www.wcw.com

World Wrestling Federation
www.wwf.com

For Further Reading

Albano, Lou, Bert Randolph Sugar, and Roger Woodson. *The Complete Idiot's Guide to Pro Wrestling.* 2nd ed. New York: Alpha Books, 2000.

Archer, Jeff. *Theater in a Squared Circle.* New York: White-Boucke Publishing, 1998.

Cohen, Dan. *Wrestling Renegades: An In-Depth Look at Today's Superstars of Pro Wrestling.* New York: Archway, 1999.

Farley, Cal. *Two Thousand Sons: The Story of Cal Farley's Boys Ranch.* Washington: Phoenix Publishing, 1987.

Hofstede, David. *Slammin': Wrestling's Greatest Heroes and Villains.* New York: ECW Press, 1999.

Mazer, Sharon. *Professional Wrestling: Sport and Spectacle.* Jackson, MS: University Press of Mississippi, 1998.

Myers, Robert. *The Professional Wrestling Trivia Book.* 2nd ed. Boston: Branden Books, 1999.

Works Cited

"Flair Defeats Race for Wrestling Title." *Greensboro Daily News,* November 25, 1983, p. D-3.

Heller, Bob. "A Flair for Wrestling." *The Charlotte Observer,* October 26, 1976.

Hodierne, Robert. "Ric Flair's Bidding for Stardom." *The Charlotte Observer,* May 30, 1976, p. F-1.

Keller, Wade. "Flair Wins NWA Title." *Pro Wrestling Torch,* July 19, 1993, p. 1.

Keller, Wade. "Ric Flair Loses Retirement Match to Hogan." *Pro Wrestling Torch*, October 29, 1994, p. 1.

"Kerry Von Erich's Three Weeks on Top of the World." *Pro Wrestling Illustrated*, October 1984, pp. 32–34.

Lacy, Mary Bishop, and Roger Mikeal. "Promoter, 3 Wrestlers Injured in Plane Crash." *The Charlotte Observer*, October 5, 1975.

Mooneyham, Mike. "Flair Firing Throws WCW, NWA into Turmoil." *The News and Courier/The Evening Post*, July 7, 1991, p. C-12.

For Further Reading

"Ric Flair's Solemn Starrcade Vow: 'If Vader Beats Me, I'll Quit Wrestling Forever.'" *World Championship Wrestling Magazine,* February 1994, pp. 40–45.

Ziegel, Vic. "The Flair for Dramatics." *Daily News,* December 22, 1993, p. 72.

Index

A
Anderson, Arn, 33–34, 54–56, 75, 76, 85, 89, 91
Anderson, Ole, 24, 33–34, 36, 54–56, 75
Austin, Steve, 9, 76

B
Battle of the Nature Boys, 25–26
battle royals, 7, 32, 68
Benoit, Chris, 38, 91
Bischoff, Eric, 90, 91
Blanchard, Tully, 33–34
Brazil, Bobo, 24

C
Clash of the Champions, 46, 51, 76, 77, 81

D
Dillon, James J., 33, 38

F
Flair, David, 91–94
Flair, Reid, 89–90
Flair, Ric
    childhood/growing up, 9, 12–15
    early wrestling days, 15–17, 19
    and fans, 10, 11, 29, 35, 42, 60, 62–63
    feud with son David, 93–94
    injuries, 7, 21–22, 47, 87
    named wrestler of the decade, 48
    named wrestler of the year, 28, 31, 60
    physical appearance of, 5, 16, 17, 19, 23
    in plane crash, 20–21
    titles won, 6–7, 8, 10, 19–20, 23, 24, 25, 26, 28, 29, 31,

Index

36, 38, 46, 56, 58, 66, 69, 73, 86, 87
wrestling losses, 6, 29, 30, 31, 36, 43, 46, 56, 63, 73, 74, 81, 83, 87
Four Horsemen, the, 33–36, 38, 42, 47, 51–56, 59, 69, 75–76, 88–89, 91
Funk, Terry, 18, 47, 48–51

G
Gagne, Verne, 15–17, 19
Great American Bash, 38–39, 50, 56

H
Hart, Bret, 66, 73–74
Hennig, Curt, 6, 38, 74, 88–89, 91
Hogan, Hulk, 6, 60, 61, 62, 63, 66–68, 69, 74, 80–83, 84–85, 88, 91

J
Jim Crockett Promotions, 17, 20, 58

L
Luger, Lex, 36, 38–39, 50, 54–56

M
McDaniel, Wahoo, 20, 22, 23, 24
Mid-Atlantic title, 19, 20, 23, 24

N
National Wrestling Alliance (NWA), 6, 17, 18, 20, 24, 25, 26, 29, 31, 34, 36, 38, 46, 47, 51, 54, 56, 58, 62, 69, 73, 86, 90
New Blood, the, 34, 93
New World Order, 34, 88, 90

P
Piper, Roddy, 62, 66, 88
Pro Wrestling Illustrated, 23, 26, 39, 48, 71

R
Race, Harley, 7, 8–9, 10, 18, 26, 29, 43, 77
Rhodes, Dusty, 26–28, 31, 35, 38, 43
Rogers, Buddy, 13, 17, 25, 71

S
Savage, Randy, 69, 71–73, 85–87
Slamboree, 75, 85, 88
Starrcade, 8, 9, 29, 56, 86
Steamboat, Rick, 11, 24, 43–46, 77
Sting, 9, 38, 50, 51–56
SuperBrawl, 75, 84–85, 86–87, 93

T
tag teams, 19–20, 24, 25, 34
Tunney, Jack, 67–68

U

Undertaker, the, 66–68

V

Vader, Big Van, 6, 7–8, 10, 77, 84–85
Vicious, Sid (Sid Justice), 38, 59, 69
Von Erich, Kerry, 30–31, 43

W

Windham, Barry, 38, 93
World Championship Wrestling (WCW), 5–6, 7, 11, 58, 59–60, 61–62, 69, 71, 73, 75, 80, 85, 86, 87, 89–91, 93
World Wrestling Federation (WWF), 6, 7, 61–62, 63, 67, 68, 69, 71, 73, 74, 80, 87
WrestleMania, 72, 74
Wrestle War, 46, 51–54

Photo Credits

All photos courtesy of *Pro Wrestling Illustrated*.

Series Design and Layout

Geri Giordano

www.ingramcontent.com/pod-product-compliance
Lightning Source LLC
Chambersburg PA
CBHW052101070526
44584CB00017B/2282